"The short junky stories of the lemmings and the grizzly"

Presentation:

Welcome to "The Brief Amusing Stories of the Lemmings and the Grizzly"! In this unconventional collection, we welcome you to set out on a delightful journey filled with chuckling, camaraderie, and extraordinary enterprises. Connect the evil lemmings and their impossible companion, the lively grizzly bear, as they explore through an arrangement of

silly adventures
within the
dynamic wild

These stories transport us to a world where the lemmings and the grizzly resist conventions and discover delight within the most unforeseen circumstances. From wacky camping misadventures to wild berry buffets, from unconventional hide-and-seek diversions to crazy spa days, each story is beyond any doubt to tickle your clever bone and leave you with a grin all over .

Within the middle of their experiences, the lemmings and the grizzly manufacture a bond established in fellowship, chuckling, and the shared interest of carefree fun. Through their tricks, they remind us of the delight that comes from grasping preposterousness, celebrating the crazy, and cherishing the company of improbable companions.

So, get a cozy spot, settle in, and plan to be whisked absent into a world where the woodland echoes with chuckling and each turn and turn guarantees a chuckle. "The Brief Clever Stories of the Lemmings and the Grizzly" welcomes you to drench yourself within the caprice of nature's play area and rediscover the control of giggling as a widespread dialect.

Are you prepared to connect the lemmings and the grizzly on their entertainingly captivating enterprises? Let's plunge in and let the giggling start!

Table of Contents:

- The Lemmings and the Baffled Bear
- The Awesome Lemming Elude
- The Entertaining Honeypot Heist
- The Wild Water Slide Experience
- The Extraordinary Berry Burglary
- The Silly Fishing Fiasco
- The Wacky Wilderness Camping
- The Great Berry Buffet
- The Hilarious Hide-and-Seek
- The Unbearably Silly Spa Day

"The Lemmings and the Baffled Bear"

Once upon a time, in an excellent timberland, there lived a gathering of gutsy lemmings. These small critters were continuously up for an unused and energizing challenge. One day, as they hurried through the timberland, they faltered upon a grizzly bear named Gerald, who was getting a charge out of a tranquil evening rest.

The lemmings, being evil and full of interest, couldn't stand up to the allurement to play a trick on Gerald. They accumulated around, whispering and laughing, and concocted a brilliant arrangement. They chose to wake up Gerald within the most entertaining way conceivable.

One courageous lemming named Larry, with a twinkle in his eye, ventured forward and said, "Tune in up, everybody! Here's what we'll do. Let's tickle Gerald's nose with a plume whereas he's resting. When he wakes up, he'll think he's wheezing so hard that he's blown himself into a tree!"

The lemmings concurred, and discreetly they snuck up to the sleeping Gerald. They carefully situated the plume right before his huge, jerking nose. With a tender bump, they tickled his nose and held up anxiously for the appearance to start.

Abruptly, Gerald's eyes flew open, and he let out a deafening wheeze that sent him tumbling in reverse. He rolled around in a daze, swatting at fanciful branches and cleared out, attempting to recapture his composure.

In the interim, the lemmings burst into chimes of chuckling, rolling on the ground and holding their modest tummies. Their arrangement had worked impeccably! They couldn't accept their luckiness.

Gerald, still a bit muddled, looked around with bewilderment. He couldn't see any tree he had as far as anyone knows flown into, and he couldn't get what had just happened. He scratched his head, shrugged his enormous shoulders, and continued his rest, choosing it was all fair a strange dream.

The lemmings, fulfilled with their fruitful trick, rushed absent, pleased of their cleverness. They knew they had brightened up Gerald's day, and they couldn't hold up to arrange their following adventure.

From that day forward, at whatever point the lemmings saw Gerald within the timberland, they couldn't offer assistance but laugh and wink at each other, knowing they shared a mystery that would until the end of time bond them together.

And so, within the charmed woodland, the evil lemmings and the befuddled grizzly bear made a fellowship built on chuckling and lively tricks, making their days brighter and their experiences more out of control than ever recently.

"The Awesome Lemming Elude"

Within the heart of the wild, where the trees whispered privileged insights and the waterways moved with bliss, a bunch of enthusiastic lemmings found a or maybe impossible to miss grizzly bear named Gracie. Gracie was known for her clumsy nature and her unquenchable craving for nectar.

One sunny morning, the evil lemmings brought forth a fiendish arrangement. They needed to witness Gracie's fixation with nectar firsthand, trusting it would lead to an engaging experience. They set out on a mission to discover the sweetest, stickiest nectar within the whole woodland.

After a broad look, the lemmings faltered upon a beekeeper's truck that stopped close to the edge of the woods. It was filled to the brim with golden jugs of luscious nectar. Fervor shone within the lemmings' eyes as they formulated their arrangement.

Unbeknownst to the lemmings, Gracie had caught a whiff of the powerful smell of nectar. She took after her nose, driving her straight to the beekeeper's truck. The location of those delicious jugs of nectar made her mouth water, and she couldn't stand up to exploring assistance.

In the meantime, the lemmings had situated themselves deliberately around the truck, prepared to put their arrangement into action. One courageous lemming, named Lucy, drew nearer Gracie and welcomed her with an excited wave.

"Hi, Gracie! We've found something unimaginable. There's a secret nectar party happening fair past those trees," Lucy shouted, indicating within the course of a covered up glade.

Gracie's eyes extended with fervor. She overlooked all almost her introductory eagerly and energetically taken after Lucy, her thundering tummy directing her each step. The lemmings, smiling underhandedly, drove her more profoundly into the timberland, taking care not to be seen.

As they arrived at the glade, the lemmings uncovered their mystery:

the glade was embellished with honey-filled blooms, the nectar overflowing from each petal. Gracie couldn't accept her luckiness and jumped right in, eating up the sweet treasure.

Unbeknownst to Gracie, the lemmings had joined a little radio to her collar, playing a catchy tune that may be listened from miles away. The energetic tune sent Gracie into a moving free for all, whirling and influencing in the midst of the honey-filled knoll.

Word of the moving bear spread quickly through the woodland, and creatures from all corners ran to witness the display. Squirrels tapped their paws, rabbits jumped along, and feathered creatures rippled within the discussion, all joining Gracie in her honey-induced move party.

The lemmings observed from a secure separate, clutching their stomachs in giggling. They had coordinated the foremost uncommon appearance the woodland had ever seen, all for the adore of nectar.

As the sun started to set, Gracie at last collapsed onto the delicate grass, her paunch full of nectar and her heart filled with bliss. The timberland animals commended and said thanks to her for the extraordinary excitement. Gracie, still feeling the honey's impacts, let out a placated bear burp and twisted up for a peaceful sleep.

The lemmings, presently having shared an extraordinary enterprise with their newly discovered companion, tiptoed absent, taking off Gracie to appreciate her honey-induced dreams.

And so, within the charmed timberland, the lemmings and Gracie made a legend of a moving bear and a never-ending cherish for nectar. Their adventure brought chuckling, delight, and a sweet memory that would be cherished until the end of time.

"The Entertaining Honeypot Heist"

Once upon a time, in a lavish woodland overflowing with life, a fiendish group of lemmings crossed paths with a or maybe impossible to miss grizzly bear named Gus. Gus had a notoriety for being the clumsiest bear within the whole forest, continuously faltering upon experiences when he slightest anticipated them.

One sunny day, as the lemmings hurried through the timberland, they faltered upon an deserted outing spot. To their surprise, they found a gigantic pot of nectar, sparkling within the daylight. The sweet smell filled the discussion, and the lemmings' modest noses jerked with charm.

Incapable of standing up to the temptation, the lemmings chose to claim the nectar for themselves. In any case, they knew that Gus had a voracious cherish for nectar as well. So, they came up with an arrangement to outmaneuver him and appreciate the brilliant treat all to themselves.

The lemmings assembled around, whispering and plotting their conspiracy. They chose to make a redirection that would bait Gus absent from the nectar pot whereas they made their move. One lemming named Larry, known for his fast thinking, proposed a brilliant thought.

Larry dashed over to an adjacent berry bush and culled a modest bunch of delicious, ready strawberries. He held them tall and yelled, "Hello, Gus! See what we found! A berry buffet fit for a bear!"

Gus, his nose jerking at the mention of berries, turned his head and saw Larry waving the strawberries within the discussion. His eyes extended with energy, and he charged toward the lemmings, overlooking all around the nectar.

In the meantime, the rest of the lemmings quickly encompassed the nectar pot, snickering and chattering with expectation. They utilized their agile paws to carry the nectar pot back to their cozy burrow, cautious not to spill a single drop.

As the lemmings celebrated their triumph, Gus devoured on the full strawberries, savoring each succulent nibble. Small did he know that his cherished nectar pot had vanished right beneath his nose.

Hours afterward, when Gus's stomach was constantly full of strawberries, he returned to the excursion spot, prepared to enjoy his nectar treasure. But to his articulate shock, the pot was no place to be found. Confounded and befuddled, he scratched his head, pondering how the nectar had vanished into lean discussion.

Back at the lemmings' burrow, the little animals savored the stolen nectar, licking their lips with charm. They clinked their smaller than expected honey-filled mugs together, toasting their effective heist.

From that day forward, at whatever point Gus passed by the lemmings, they would share undercover smiles and smothered chuckling, knowing they had pulled off the extreme nectar pot caper right beneath his nose.

And so, within the heart of the woodland, the evil lemmings and the bumbling Gus made an amazing story of a nectar pot heist, filled with chuckling, guile,and a sweet triumph that would be whispered among the woodland animals for eras to come.

"The Wild Water Slide Experience"

In a dynamic woodland where chuckling resounded through the trees, a bunch of energetic lemmings set out on a silly adventure with their impossible companion, an adorable grizzly bear named Benny. Benny was known for his clumsiness and his consistent longing for salmon.

One sunny day, as the lemmings hurried along the riverbank, they perched upon a towering waterfall. Their insidious minds started to spin with thoughts, and they chose to turn the waterfall into a terrific water slide for their beguilement.

Enthusiastically, the lemmings started developing a slide made of clears out and twigs, bending and turning down the slant, driving to the waterway underneath. It was a showstopper of their inventiveness, and they couldn't hold up to see the expressions on their friends' faces.

They accumulated around Benny, who was happily looking at the sparkling water. The lemmings, smiling from ear to ear, shared their bright arrangement with Benny.

"Benny, our expensive companion, we have something uncommon to appear to you," announced Lucy, the pioneer of the lemmings. "We've made a water slide fair for you! Get prepared for the most out of control ride of your life!"

Benny's eyes extended with fervor, his paws shivering at the thought of sliding down the wonderful waterfall. Small did he know what he was almost to encounter.

With an evil flicker in their eyes, the lemmings situated Benny at the best of the slide. They gave him a tender thrust, and off he went, tearing down the watery way.

As Benny plummeted, his hide unsettled by the surging water, he let out a pleased thunder. But fair as he thought the enterprise couldn't get any way better, he slammed into a bend and veered off course, flying through the discussion some time recently diving into an adjacent shrubbery of bushes.

The lemmings couldn't contain their giggling as they observed Benny develop from the bushes, secured in takes off and twigs, his dazed expression coordinating their possessed entertainment.

Resolute by his startling reroute, Benny shook off the flotsam and jetsam, radiating with fervor. He couldn't hold up to handle the water slide once more.

Circular after circular, Benny zipped down the slide, experiencing startling turns and turns each time. Now and then he would take off through the discussion like a clumsy gymnastic performer, whereas other times he would turn in circles, some time recently landing in a heap of quills from a astounded run of ducks.

The timberland creatures, drawn by the commotion, assembled around the riverbank to witness Benny's comical water slide enterprise. They giggled, cheered, and clapped their paws and wings in charm.

After a few invigorating rides and incalculable paunch snickers, Benny at long last rose from the water, triumphant but drenched to the bone. The lemmings, praising his bravery and grasping his soul of experience, assembled around him in celebration.

From that day forward, at whatever point Benny and the lemmings crossed ways, they couldn't offer assistance but think back almost their wild water slide experience. It became a cherished memory, until the end of time carved in their hearts and retold with chuckling within the heart of the timberland.

And so, within the unusual forest, the brave lemmings and the adorable Benny shared a bond fashioned through giggling and the excitement of unforeseen experiences, making a story of fellowship and entertaining adventures that would resound through the woodland for eras to come.

"The Extraordinary Berry Burglary"

In a pleasant glade settled among towering trees, a fiendish pack of lemmings set out on a comical caper with their impossible accomplice, a neighborly grizzly bear named Barry. Barry was known for his voracious craving for berries and his talent for getting himself into silly pickles.

One sunny morning, as the lemmings rushed through the glade, their minor eyes caught the location of a bountiful berry fix. The delicious, ready berries called to them, essentially asking to be eaten up. But there was one problem—the berries were protected by a towering fence, apparently outlandish for the small lemmings to overcome.

But where there's a will, there's a way, and the lemmings were decided to fulfill their berry desires. They are drawn closer to Barry, their intelligent minds buzzing with a brassy arrangement.

"Barry, expensive companion, we have a berry crisis!" squeaked Lucy, the pioneer of the lemmings. "The berry fix is fenced off, and we require your offer assistance to devour on those luscious berries. Can you help us with the most prominent berry burglary this knoll has ever seen?"

Barry's eyes shone with evil as he tuned in to the lemmings' task. He adored a great enterprise, particularly in case it included his cherished berries. Without hesitation, he concurred to assist the lemmings execute their brave arrangement.

The lemmings hurried around, gathering supplies and building a temporary step made of twigs and taking off. They inclined the stepping stool against the fence, making a way to bury heaven. Barry, being the most grounded among them, climbed the stepping stool with ease, his expectation developing with each step.

With an extraordinary hurl, Barry raised himself over the fence, landing on the other side with a crash. The lemmings, holding up restlessly underneath, cheered him on with their minor voices.

But fair as Barry was approximately to jump into the ocean of berries, catastrophe struck. The step collapsed beneath his weight, clearing out the lemmings stranded on one side of the fence whereas their accomplice was caught in the midst of the berry bounty.

The lemmings squeaked in freeze, their minor paws scrambling to discover an arrangement. They realized they were required to come up with a way to protect Barry and, of course, secure their berry devour.

Considered rapidly, the lemmings formed a chain, standing on each other's shoulders to make a tower of lemming control. It wobbled unstably, but they decided to reach their berry-loving companion.

With a last jump, the best lemming overseen to get a handle on the edge of the fence, pulling Barry to security with a collective exertion. The lemmings and Barry tumbled in reverse, landing in a pile of chuckling and alleviation.

In the midst of the chaos, they realized they had accomplished their goal—the berries were theirs for the taking. They ate up the juicy natural products, juice recoloring their hide and filling their paunches with fruity charm.

From that day forward, at whatever point the lemmings and Barry passed by the berry fix, they couldn't offer assistance but share evil smiles, reviewing their extraordinary berry burglary and the triumph over the imposing fence.

And so, within the heart of the glade, the courageous lemmings and the berry-loving Barry got to be incredible figures, their story of cooperation, chuckling, and a shared cherish for berries until the end of time carved within the recollections of the meadow's occupants.

"The Silly Fishing Fiasco"

In an unconventional woodland where chuckling moved among the trees, a fiendish group of lemmings found themselves ensnared in a comical venture with their impossible companion, a clumsy grizzly bear named Gilbert. Gilbert was known for his cherish of angling and his talent for entertaining angling disasters.

One sunny day, as the lemmings skipped close to a peaceful lake, they perched upon Gilbert, who was endeavoring to capture angle with his trusty angling pole. The lemmings couldn't stand up to the opportunity for a few laughter-filled amusement and chose to connect Gilbert in his calculating enterprise.

In any case, the lemmings had a lively trap up their sleeves. They furtively tied an elastic duck to the conclusion of Gilbert's angling line when he wasn't looking, swapping it with his standard snare. The lemmings stowed away behind adjacent bushes, enthusiastic to witness the exhibition unfurl.

With a determined expression on his confrontation, Gilbert cast his line into the gleaming waters, anticipating to capture an angle in no time. Small did he know that an astonish anticipated him at the conclusion of his line.

As he sat calmly, the line abruptly jerked and squirmed. Gilbert's eyes broadened with expectation, envisioning a colossal angle at the other conclusion. With all his might, he yanked the angling bar upward, bracing himself for a powerful battle.

To his wonder, rather than at an angle, a squeaky elastic duck took off through the discussion, landing with a comical sprinkle right before him. Gilbert flickered in disarray, his textured eyebrows furrowing with bewilderment.

In the interim, the lemmings burst into wild fits of giggling, their minor bodies shaking with gaiety. They rolled on the ground, clutching their stomachs, incapable of containing their entertainment at the startling result.

Gilbert, at first puzzled, soon found himself chuckling together with the lemmings. His genuine angling undertaking had turned into an entertaining exhibition, and he couldn't offer assistance but appreciate the lemmings' evil sense of humor.

Unfazed by the elastic duck occurrence, Gilbert chose to grant angling another shot. He cast his line into the water once once more, decided to recover himself and capture a real angel this time.

The lemmings, observing eagerness, held their breath in expectation. But destiny had a diverse arrangement in store. As Gilbert pulled his angling pole with extraordinary excitement, the line got tangled in an adjacent tree department. The lemmings' eyes broadened, and they traded evil looks.

With an inadvertently comical expression of assurance, Gilbert pulled at the angling bar, attempting to free it from the department. In an instant, the department snapped back, causing Gilbert to lose his adjust and arrive with a powerful sprinkle within the lake, angling pole and all.

The lemmings ejected into wild giggling, their high-pitched snickers resounding through the woodland. Gilbert, splashed but still chuckling, swam back to the shore, joining the lemmings in their mirth-filled party.

From that day forward, at whatever point the lemmings and Gilbert assembled by the lakeside, they couldn't offer assistance but review the senseless angling disaster that had brought them so much delight. It became a cherished memory, until the end of time carved in their hearts and shared with chuckling within the heart of the woodland.

And so, within the unusual forest, the fiendish lemmings and the good-hearted Gilbert made a story of companionship, giggling, and exceptional angling disasters, guaranteeing that their bond would persevere through numerous more comical experiences to come.

"The Wacky Wilderness Camping"

In a lavish wild where chuckling resounded through the trees, an evil bunch of lemmings set out on a silly camping enterprise with their improbable companion, a delicate grizzly bear named Gracie. Gracie was known for her cherish of picnics and her clumsy nature that frequently drove her to interesting circumstances.

One sunny end of the week, the lemmings decided it was time for a camping trip to investigate the awesome outside. Enthusiastically, they stuffed their smaller than expected rucksacks with snacks, camping equipment, and an excess of marshmallows for simmering over the campfire.

As the lemmings set up their modest tents, Gracie stumbled over, charmed by the prospect of joining their wild venture. The lemmings, continuously open to modern encounters, invited her with open arms, knowing that Gracie's nearness would include a touch of entertainment to their camping experience.

Little did they know that Gracie had never been camping some time recently, and her need of open air mastery would before long lead to uproarious occasions.

The lemmings accumulated around the campfire, sharing stories and simmering marshmallows to flawlessness. Gracie, enthusiastic to take part, endeavored to broil her marshmallow by holding it specifically in her paw over the open fire.

Obviously, the marshmallow caught fire, overwhelming Gracie's paw in a burst. Freezing, she quickly waved her paw, accidentally sending flaring marshmallows flying through the discussion. The lemmings ducked and evaded the red hot shots, their squeaks of astonish changing into chimes of chuckling.

Unfazed by her marshmallow incident, Gracie chose to recover herself by illustrating her angling aptitudes. Outfitted with an angling bar borrowed from one of the lemmings, she swam into an adjacent stream, decided to capture an angle for supper.

In any case, Gracie's angling endeavors turned into a droll exhibition. With each cast of her angling bar, she overseen to snare her claim hide, a stray tree department, and indeed one of the lemmings' rucksacks. The lemmings observed in entertainment as Gracie's angling ventures got to be a silly show of tangled lines and unforeseen catches.

As sunset settled, the lemmings and Gracie withdrew to their tents for a night of rest beneath the starry sky. In any case, Gracie's tent-pitching aptitudes were less than stellar. With each endeavor, her tent collapsed, clearing out her tangled in a mess of texture and shafts. The lemmings couldn't contain their giggling as they observed Gracie's tireless endeavors to overcome the wild tent.

At last, depleted from the day's misadventures, Gracie surrendered to the chaos, sprawling out on the grass, utilizing her hide as a temporary resting sack. The lemmings, in an appeal of solidarity, joined her, cuddling against her warm and feathery side.

Underneath the twinkling stars, in the midst of the giggling and shared camaraderie, the lemmings and Gracie found delight in their unusual camping trip. The disasters and laughter-filled minutes got to be cherished recollections, until the end of time carved in their hearts.

And so, within the heart of the wild, the insidious lemmings and the good-hearted Gracie made a story of companionship, chuckling, and exceptional camping calamities. Their bond developed more grounded with each entertaining venture, guaranteeing that their wild experiences would be filled with delight and uproarious giggling for a long time to come.

"The Great Berry Buffet"

In a dynamic woodland where chuckling reverberated among the trees, an evil group of lemmings set out on a divertingly chaotic travel with their improbable accomplice, a food-loving grizzly bear named Gourmet. Gourmet was known for his unquenchable craving and his talent for finding the foremost luscious treats within the wild.

One sunny day, as the lemmings rushed through the undergrowth, their modest eyes caught sight of a sprawling berry fix. The bushes were bursting with stout, succulent berries of each color possible. The lemmings' paunches thundered with expectation, and they couldn't stand up to the appeal of the berry buffet.

Unbeknownst to them, Gourmet was moreover adjacent, his nose jerking with the fragrance of juicy berries. The lemmings, energetic to share their disclosure, called out to Gourmet, welcoming him to connect their berry devour.

Gourmet, incapable to stand up to the guarantee of a scrumptious supper, enthusiastically taken after the lemmings to the berry fix. Their arrangement was basic: each lemming would assemble berries and hurl them to Gourmet, who would capture them in his enormous paws and enjoy to his heart's substance.

Fervor filled the discussion as the lemmings culled berries and tossed them one by one towards Gourmet. The primary few tosses went easily, with Gourmet deftly catching the berries in mid-air and eating them up with fervor.

In any case, as the lemmings developed more energized and their hurling got quicker, chaos followed. Berries flew in all bearings, lost their target completely or bounced off Gourmet's nose. The lemmings couldn't offer assistance but burst into fits of chuckling at the ridiculousness of the circumstance.

Gourmet, unfazed by the berry assault, opened his mouth wide, endeavoring to capture as numerous berries as conceivable. The lemmings seized the opportunity, throwing handfuls of berries at him, causing a blast of colorful natural product within the discussion.

Berries cruised through the woodland like minor shots, landing within the branches of adjacent trees, covering the lemmings' hide, and indeed splattering the faces of other woodland creatures passing by. The woodland became an unconventional front line of berries.

Through the berry chaos, the lemmings and Gourmet thundered with chuckling, their stomachs hurting from jollity. They couldn't offer assistance but wonder at the ridiculousness of their offhand berry hurling free for all.

At last, depleted and covered in berry stains, the lemmings and Gourmet collapsed onto the grass, their giggling resounding through the timberland. They revealed within the memory of the berry buffet gone astray, their hearts filled with shared bliss and extraordinary camaraderie.

From that day forward, at whatever point the lemmings and Gourmet experienced a berry fix, they couldn't offer assistance but review the riotous berry buffet that had brought them so much chuckling. It became a cherished memory, until the end of time carved in their hearts and shared with chuckles within the heart of the timberland.

And so, within the unusual forest, the fiendish lemmings and the food-loving Gourmetmade a story of companionship, chuckling, and the journey for the extreme berry devour. Their bond developed more grounded with each entertaining adventure, guaranteeing that their timberland experiences would continuously be accompanied with chimes of giggling and the sweet taste of shared recollections.

"The Hilarious Hide-and-Seek"

In an exuberant glade where giggling blossomed like wildflowers, a fiendish pack of lemmings found themselves caught in an unusual amusement of hide-and-seek with their improbable companion, a lively grizzly bear named Benny. Benny was known for his cherish of diversions and his mysterious capacity to create any movement entertainingly engaging.

One sunny afternoon, the lemmings assembled within the glade, their minor eyes shimmering with evil charm. They crouched together, plotting their another lively enterprise. That's when Benny, with a happy twinkle in his eyes, proposed an amusement of hide-and-seek.

Fervor undulated through the lemmings as they concurred to Benny's recommendation. They rapidly set up the rules: Benny would tally to ten while the lemmings hurried to find stowing away spots, and after that Benny would seek for them.

With a fiendish smile, Benny secured his eyes and started to tally. "One, two, three..." he chanted, giving the lemmings fair sufficient time to vanish into the meadow's alcoves and corners.

Benny wrapped up tallying and yelled, "Prepared or not, here I come!" He charged forward, sniffing the discussion and filtering the knoll for any signs of the covered up lemmings.

Unbeknownst to Benny, the lemmings had formulated a "arrange blend up">to blend up and astonish their lively followers. They dashed almost, quickly swapping covering up spots at whatever point Benny drew close, their minor snickers resounding through the knoll.

Benny, decided to discover the lemmings, clumsily looked

underneath bushes, looked behind trees, and indeed jabbed his nose into empty logs. Each time he thought he had spotted a lemming, it turned out to be a leaf or a cleverly camouflaged shake.

The lemmings, covered up adjacent, couldn't contain their chuckling. They observed with merriment as Benny's endeavors to discover them developed progressively comical. At one point, Benny mixed up a passing butterfly for a lemming and jumped on it, as it were to conclude up with a sizable chunk of vacillating wings and a perplexed expression.

As Benny proceeded his passionate look, the lemmings chose to require their silliness to the another level. They worked together, subtly orchestrating themselves in a push behind a fallen log, disguising themselves as a single long, fuzzy animal.

Benny, decided to discover the lemmings, faltered upon the camouflaged push of lemmings behind the log. With a triumphant thunder, he lurched forward, prepared to capture the entire "animal" in one swoop.

But much to Benny's astonishment, the lemmings scattered in all bearings, revealing themselves to be a gathering of partitioned people. They squeaked with giggling as Benny stood there, confused, his paw hanging in mid-air.

The glade emitted with uproarious chuckling as Benny joined within the cheer, recognizing the lemmings' intelligent trick. They revealed within the happy craziness of the hide-and-seek amusement, their sides throbbing from giggling and their hearts filled with the warmth of shared beguilement.

From that day forward, at whatever point the lemmings and Benny accumulated within the glade, they couldn't offer assistance but review the wild hide-and-seek diversion that had brought them so much chuckling. It became a cherished memory, until the end of time carved in their hearts and shared with chuckles within the heart of the knoll.

And so, in the unusual glade, the mischievous lemmings and the perky Benny made a story of companionship, chuckling, and the delight of shared diversions. Their bond developed more grounded with each silly adventure, guaranteeing that their knoll enterprises would continuously be gone with chimes of giggling and the bliss of lively camaraderie.

"The Unbearably Silly Spa Day"

In an exuberant woodland where chuckling reverberated through the trees, an evil bunch of lemmings set out on a divertingly wacky spa day with their improbable companion, a laid-back grizzly bear named Bubbles. Bubbles was known for his adore of unwinding and his talent for turning standard exercises into uproarious enterprises.

One sunny evening, as the lemmings skipped close to a chattering tolerance, they faltered upon Bubbles sluggishly relaxing in the midst of an improvised spa setup. Interested by the guarantee of spoiling, the lemmings enthusiastically drew nearer him, inquisitive to involvement in the unconventional spa medicines.

Bubbles, with a twinkle in his eye, invited the lemmings to his timberland spa to withdraw. He guaranteed them a day filled with unwinding and giggling, where they might loosen up and enjoy the most ridiculous spa ceremonies possible.

The lemmings, continuously up for a great giggle, concurred without faltering. They settled down on delicate greenery pads and prepared themselves for the foremost unusual spa involvement of their lives.

Bubbles, the ace spa master, started by offering the lemmings a reviving facial treatment. Rather than cucumbers, he put cuts of succulent watermelon on their modest faces. The lemmings snickered as the sticky natural product made them see more like fruity veils than spa-goers.

Another up was a foot rub like no other. Bubbles, utilizing his monster paws, delicately worked the lemmings' minor feet, sending them into fits of sensitive giggling. They squirmed and squirmed, incapable to contain their silliness at the ridiculousness of a grizzly bear giving foot rubs.

But the highlight of the spa day was the bubble shower event. Bubbles poured abundant sums of bubble arrangement into a monster wooden tub and welcomed the lemmings to plunge right in. With enchanted squeaks, the lemmings jumped into the mountain of bubbles, vanishing from location.

Bubbles, joining the fun, dove headfirst into the ocean of bubbles, vanishing underneath the froth. The timberland filled with chuckling as the lemmings and Bubbles popped up sporadically, secured in bubbly facial hair and laughing wildly.

As the spa day proceeded, the lemmings and Bubbles reveled in laughter-filled yoga sessions, where tree postures turned into toppling towers, and downward-facing mutts got to be entertaining nose-to-nose encounters. They extended, tumbled, and snickered their way through each posture, revealing within the bliss of their flighty spa exercises.

With the setting sun casting a warm gleam over the woodland, the lemmings and Bubbles concluded their uproarious spa day. They assembled in a circle, their hearts filled with chuckling and camaraderie. They realized that giggling and shared nonsensicalness were the genuine fixings for a delightful spa encounter.

From that day forward, at whatever point the lemmings and Bubbles met by the tolerate, they couldn't offer assistance but review the exceptional, endurable spa day that had brought them so much laughter. It became a cherished memory, until the end of time carved in their hearts and shared with chuckles within the heart of the timberland.

And so, within the unusual forest, the fiendish lemmings and the laid-back Bubbles made a story of companionship, chuckling, and the delight of grasping nonsensicalness. Their bond developed more grounded with each silly venture, guaranteeing that their timberland enterprises would continuously be went with by chimes of chuckling and the shared recollections of their tolerably senseless spa day.

Printed in Great Britain
by Amazon